# Sea Fishing Venues
# In Wales

This book contains complete descriptions
of sea fishing venues in
NORTH WALES

I have fished the Welsh Coastline for over 25 years and have written this book with purely the sea angler in mind, who like myself live too far away from the coast to go fishing every weekend. Hopefully I have produced the most fully comprehensive guide you will ever need to help you enjoy the wonderful fishing this stretch of coastline holds.

Shore Fishing is extremely popular in Wales and, with such a large area of coastline, you can always find a quiet sheltered spot for a good days fishing.

I have pin pointed 24 well established venues with over 73 fishing marks shown on the maps. I have also shown topography maps to give you a good idea of the ground you are fishing.

Each venue offers car parking, in addition to some other amenities and all have breath-taking views out to sea. The variety of catch can be very wide and varies throughout each of the seasons. It includes Bass, Bull Huss, Coalfish, Cod, Conger Eel, Dab, Dogfish, Flounder, Mackerel, Mullet, Plaice, Pollack, Rays, including Thornback, Smalleyed, Spotted and Blonde, Smoothhound, Whiting and plenty of good size Wrasse which run to over 4lbs at times.

Also in this guide you will find additional information on baits, how to get to each of the venues, and also how to fish them and much more.

Everything at the time of writing this book is correct.

Enjoy the book and of course - **TIGHT LINES**!!!

CW01335773

# North Wales Venues Map

# Venues

1  CONNAHS QUAY (DOCK ROAD)
2  FLINT CASTLE
3  FLINT COB
4  GREENFIELD TRENCH
5  MOSTYN
6  TALACRE
7  PRESTATYN (FFRITH BEACH)
8  RHYL (SPLASH POINT)
9  KINMEL BAY
10  PENSARN
11  LLANDULLAS
12  COLWYN BAY (THE ARCHES)

13  RHOS ON SEA
14  PENRHYN BAY
15  LLANDUDNO (ANGEL BAY)
16  LLANDUDNO (NORTH SHORE)
17  LLANDUDNO (PIER)
18  LLANDUDNO (PIGEON HOLES)
19  DEGANWY
20  CONWAY
21  PEMMAENMAWR
22  LLANFAIRFECHAN
23  PORT PENRHYN
24  BANGOR PIER

# Accessibility & Comfort

**Accessibility**
1. Suitable for disabled person.
2. A short walk over light terrain.
3. Lengthy or strenuous walk over medium terrain.
4. Lengthy walk over medium terrain with scramble to fishing platform.
5. Lengthy strenuous walk with scramble to fishing platform.

**Comfort**
1. Promenade or pier.
2. Shingle or sand.
3. Boulders or stones and possibly slippery.
4. Comfortable rock platform
5. Uncomfortable rock platform.

# CONNAHS QUAY (DOCK ROAD)

## How To Get There

From Chester head on the A55 to North Wales. Turn right at Ewloe on to the A494 and then left at the Queensferry roundabout. From here travel straight on for about 2 ½ miles and turn right at Tyre Save into Dock Road. Carry on around the bends and you come to the main Dock on your left where you can fish from right by your car.

Grid Ref SJ 296697

## How To Fish

This venue is predominantly known as a great place for Flatties. Using lugworm as bait on a spoon rig has always caught lots of good size Flounder and Plaice to 2lbs. Also here you will catch Silver Eels, the odd Bass and even a rare Sea Trout

In the winter you now get a large run of Codling to 3lbs caught on lugworm wrapped in squid, Whiting to fish baits and also the occasional Bass.

Do not fish here after heavy rain or snow for the fresh water coming down from the hills kills the fishing. The river also has a Bore which on a spring tide can be quite large. This venue is best fished on a 24-25ft tide.

# CONNAHS QUAY (DOCK ROAD)

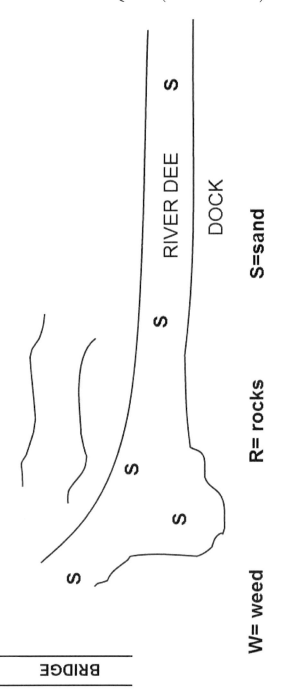

RIVER DEE

DOCK

S=sand

R= rocks

W= weed

BRIDGE

# CONNAHS QUAY (DOCK ROAD)

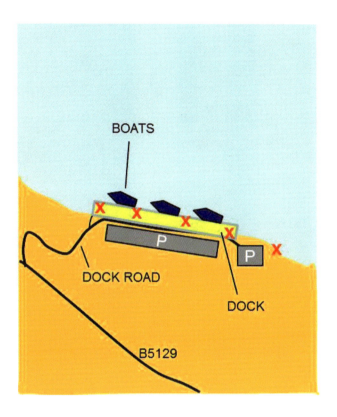

**Parking and Walking** …...Park on the Dock and you can fish straight from the car.

**Summer Species** ………. Flounder, Plaice, Whiting, Silver Eel, Bass, Sea Trout.

**Winter Species**……...…….Flounder, Plaice, Codling, Whiting, Silver Eel, Strap Conger Bass.

**Best Months**……...……...Sept – April.

**Rigs** …………….……...… 2 hook loose 1/0, Flounder Spoon 1/0.

**Best Baits**………..….........Lugworm, squid, mackerel.

---

A very strong tidal run here so best fished on a 24 - 25ft tide.

---

**Access 1     Comfort 1**

# FLINT CASTLE

How To Get There

From Chester head on the A55 to North Wales. Turn right at Ewloe on to the A494 and then left at the Queensferry roundabout onto the A548. From here travel straight on for about 5 miles and turn right when you see the sign for the Lifeboat Station. Follow this road, go past the castle and turn right and then an immediate left. Go down this road and park by the kissing gate on the right. From here follow the route to the river. It's a 5 minute walk.

Grid Ref SJ 244733

How To Fish

A Flattie venue again. Flounders and Plaice are the main targets here. Don't overcast as the fish here can be caught from as little as 10yds out. The best bait for these is lugworm. You will also get Bass to ragworm in the summer and also the odd Thornback Ray and plenty of Silver Eels.

In the winter you get the Cod run going up the river where you will catch them to 3lbs on lug tipped with squid. You will also get plenty of Whiting to fish baits and Dabs to worm.

Do not fish here after heavy rain or snow for the fresh water coming down from the hills kills the fishing. The river also has a Bore which on a spring tide can be quite large. This venue is best fished on a 24-25ft tide.

# FLINT CASTLE

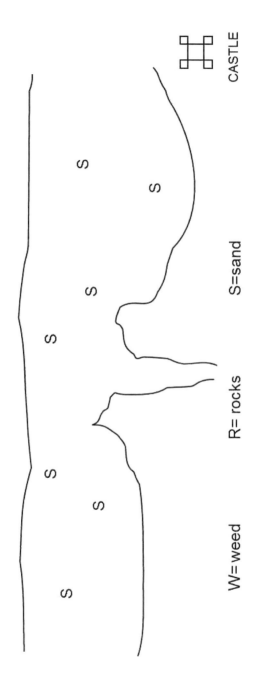

# FLINT CASTLE

**Parking and Walking** …...Park by the kissing gate and a 5 minute walk to the fishing.
**Summer Species** …….. Flounder, Plaice, Whiting, Silver Eel, Bass, Sea Trout.
**Winter Species**……..…….Flounder, Plaice, Codling, Whiting, Silver Eel, Strap Conger Bass.
**Best Months**……..……..Sept – April.
**Rigs** …………….……......2 hook loose 1/0, Flounder Spoon 1/0.
**Best Baits**……….…..........Lugworm, squid, mackerel.

Ideal here for Flatties.

**Access 1    Comfort 1**

# FLINT COB

How To Get There

From Chester head on the A55 to North Wales. Turn right at Ewloe on to the A494 and then left at the Queensferry roundabout on the A548. From here travel continue straight on and pass through Flint. Drive past McDonalds on the left and you will see the HSS Hire shop on your right. Turn right here and park up . Follow the footpath to the right of HSS, go over the railway line and you will come to the river. Here you have a large flat grass bank to fish from but this is getting smaller each year.

Grid Ref SJ 238740

How To Fish

This venue goes straight out to sea and when the tide comes in can be very windy indeed. Plaice and Dab all caught on worm baits, but best using a spoon rig with a 1/0 hook. Although the main target, other species such as Bass are caught on sandeel and rag along with Strap Conger to fish baits. Also you get the odd Thornback ray putting in an appearance and of course the resident Whiting in the winter. In the right conditions you will also catch  Cod to 4lbs.

Do not fish here after heavy rain or snow for the fresh water coming down from the hills kills the fishing. The river also has a Bore which on a spring tide can be quite large.  This venue is best fished on a 24-25ft tide.

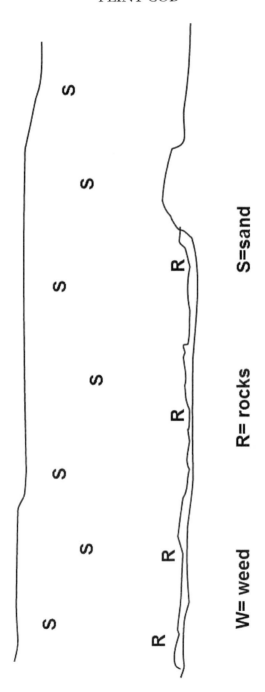

S=sand

R= rocks

W= weed

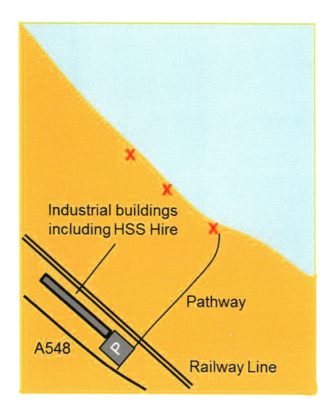

**Parking and Walking** …....Park your car next to HSS and follow the footpath to the right. It's a 10 minute walk to the fishing.
**Summer Species** ………. Flounder, Plaice, Whiting, Silver Eel, Bass.
**Winter Species**……..……..Flounder, Plaice, Codling, Whiting, Silver Eel, Strap Conger, Bass.
**Best Months**……..……..Sept – April.
**Rigs** ………….……....… 2 hook loose 1/0, Flounder Spoon 1/0.
**Best Baits**……..….........Lugworm, squid, mackerel.

---

**Wide open to the elements here but good Flattie Fishing.**

---

**Access 2    Comfort 3**

# GREENFIELD TRENCH

How To Get There

From Chester head on the A55 to North Wales. Turn right at Ewloe
on to the A494 and then left at the Queensferry roundabout on the
A548. From here travel continue straight on and pass through Flint.
As you enter Greenfield you go under the bridge and take your first
right next to the pub. Carry on down this road to the car park

Grid Ref SJ 296697

How To Fish

Another Flattie venue. Again this location, sometimes called the Trench
is made for Flounder, Plaice and Dab all caught on worm baits, but best
using a spoon rig with a 1/0 hook. Although the main target, other
species such as Bass are caught on sandeel and rag along with Strap
Conger to fish baits. Also you get the odd Thornback ray putting in an
appearance and of course the resident Whiting in the winter. In the
right conditions you will also catch plenty of Cod to 4lbs.

Do not fish here after heavy rain or snow for the fresh water coming
down from the hills kills the fishing. The river also has a Bore which on
a spring tide can be quite large. This venue is best fished on a 24-25ft
tide.

# GREENFIELD TRENCH

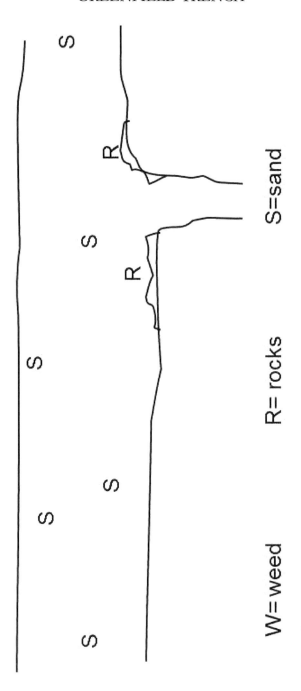

# GREENFIELD TRENCH

**Parking and Walking** …...Park in the car park and you can fish straight from the car or a short walk to the left.
**Summer Species** ………. Flounder, Plaice, Whiting, Silver Eel, Bass.
**Winter Species**……...…….Flounder, Plaice, Codling, Whiting, Silver Eel, Strap Conger, Bass.
**Best Months**……..……...Sept – April.
**Rigs** …………….…….....… 2 hook loose 1/0, Flounder Spoon 1/0.
**Best Baits**…………...........Lugworm, squid, mackerel.

Great for Flounder and Plaice.

**Access  2    Comfort  4**

16

# MOSTYN

How To Get There

From Chester head on the A55 to North Wales. Turn right at Ewloe on to the A494 and then left at the Queensferry roundabout on the A548. From here travel continue straight on for about 12 miles passing through Flint and Greenfield. When you enter Mostyn look for the Clock Tower and turn right opposite through a gate. Follow this rough road over the bridge to the top where you can park your car. Fishing is just over the wall.

Grid Ref SJ 296697

How To Fish

Best fished 1hr before to 1hr after high tide. Well known for catching Flounder, Plaice and Dabs on worm baits. This venue fishes its socks off in the daylight and when conditions are right there are plenty of Codling and Whiting to be caught. Also here you get plenty of Strap Conger when fishing close in with large fish baits. In the summer you get the odd Thornback Ray being caught on sandeel and fish baits. Do not fish here after heavy rain or snow for the fresh water coming down from the hills kills the fishing. The river also has a Bore which on a spring tide can be quite large. This venue is best fished on a 24-25ft tide.

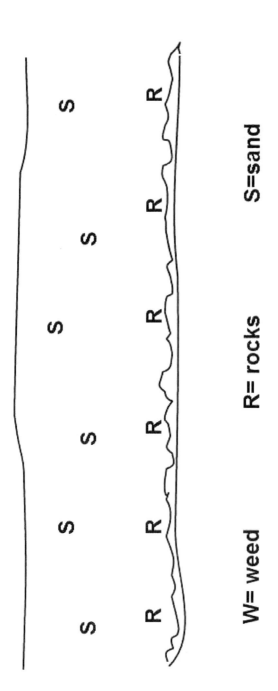

S=sand

R= rocks

W= weed

# MOSTYN

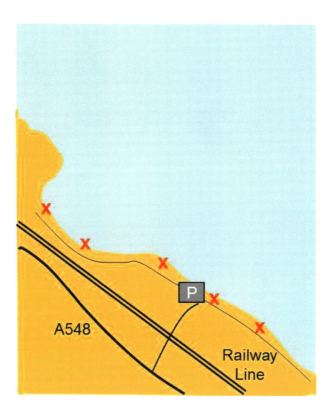

**Parking and Walking** …...Park in the car park and you can fish over the wall from the car.

**Summer Species** ………. Flounder, Plaice, Whiting, Silver Eel, Bass.

**Winter Species**……...……Flounder, Plaice, Codling, Whiting, Silver Eel, Strap Conger Bass.

**Best Months**……..……...Sept – April.

**Rigs** …………..……...… 2 hook loose 1/0, Flounder Spoon 1/0.

**Best Baits**…………........Lugworm, squid, mackerel, sandeel.

---

A very strong tidal run here so best fished on a 24 - 25ft tide.

---

Access 2    Comfort 3

# TALACRE

How To Get There

From Chester head on the A55 to North Wales. Turn right at Ewloe on to the A494 and then left at the Queensferry roundabout on the A548. From here travel continue straight on for about 15 miles passing through Flint and Greenfield. When you get to the Point of Ayr Gas Terminal roundabout, turn right. Follow this road right to the end where you can park on the beach.

Grid Ref SJ 296697

How To Fish

This is best fished either side of low water. Lots of matches get run from here and Dabs and Plaice are in abundance caught on lug and ragworm. You also catch plenty of Bass to ragworm and sandeel, and in the winter you will get large Whiting and Codling to 4lbs.

BEWARE. If fishing this venue at night time, take a compass with you. The sea mist comes in and the tide comes in around the back of you, cutting you off. Always fish in the daylight first to get to know the area.

# TALACRE

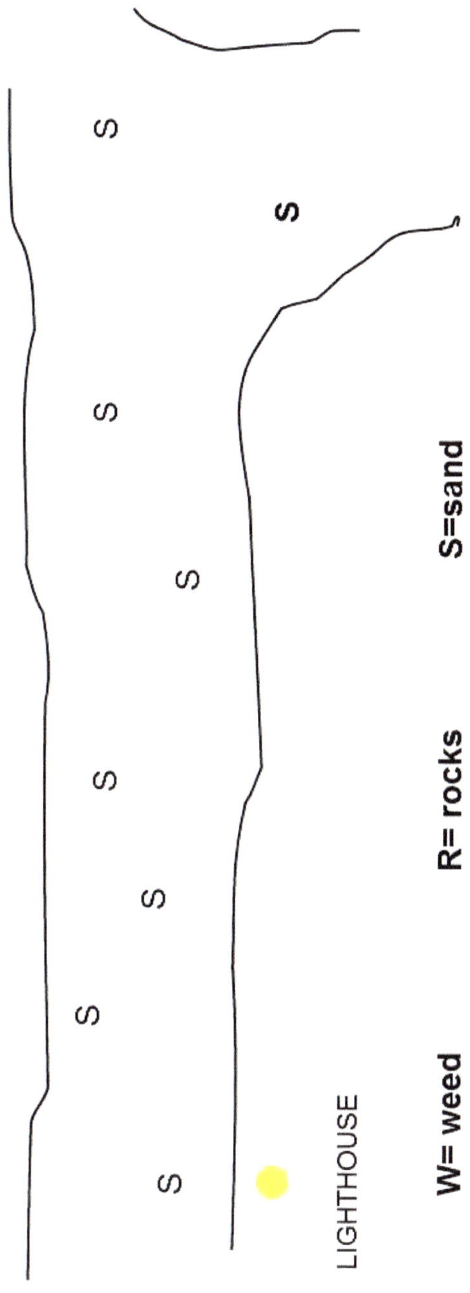

S

**S**

S

S

S

S

S

S

**S=sand**

**R= rocks**

**W= weed**

LIGHTHOUSE

# TALACRE

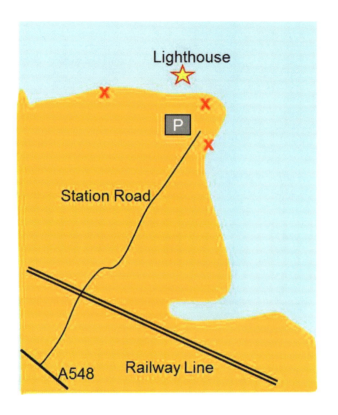

**Parking and Walking** …...Park on the beach by the sand dunes. Fishing is a ten minute walk at low water.

**Summer Species** ………. Dabs, Plaice, Flounder, Bass, Thornback Ray, Silver Eels.

**Winter Species**……..…….Codling, Whiting, Dabs, Flounder, Silver Eels.

**Best Months**…….………..Sept – May.

**Rigs** ………….….…....… 2 hook loose 1/0, Flounder Spoon 1/0.

**Best Baits**………..…..........Lugworm, Ragworm, squid, mackerel, crab.

Watch out for sea mist, sinking sand and the tide coming in behind you.

Access 3 Comfort 2

# PRESTATYN (FFRITH BEACH)

## How To Get There

Travel along the A548 from Chester. Go past Prestatyn Sands Holiday Centre and turn right at Ffrith Beach into the car park. Go to the far end and you will find a gate leading to over the sand dunes. Fish from here.

Grid Ref SJ 064829

## How To Fish

This venue is best fished at high water with a good surf. This is a nice sandy beach with no snags. In the summer Bass are the main target and can be caught up to 6lbs using ragworm as bait. Also you will catch Thornback Rays and Whiting to fish baits, Dabs and Plaice to worm baits.

In the winter you will get Codling, Whiting, Dogfish, Dabs and Rockling to worm and fish baits.

# PRESTATYN (FFRITH BEACH)

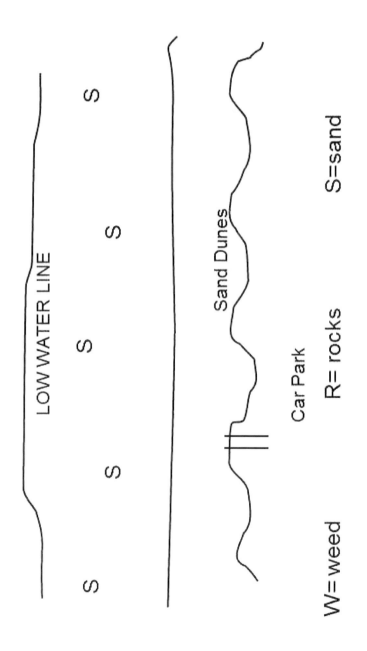

LOW WATER LINE

S  S  S  S  S

Sand Dunes

Car Park

W= weed    R= rocks    S=sand

# PRESTATYN (FFRITH BEACH)

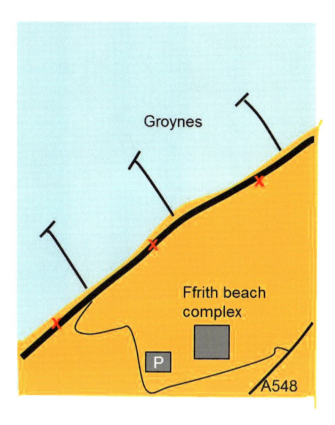

**Parking and Walking** …...Park in the car park at the far end. Go through the gate, over the dunes and fish here.

**Summer Species** ………. Bass, Thornback Rays, Plaice, Dabs, Silver Eel.

**Winter Species**……..……..Codling, Whiting, Dabs, Flounder, Silver Eels.

**Best Months**……..……...Sept – Dec.

**Rigs** ………….……...…. 2 and 3 hook Clip Down 1/0,

**Best Baits**……..…..….......Lugworm, Ragworm, squid, mackerel, crab, sandeel.

---

Some good Bass can be caught here on Lugworm.

---

**Access 2    Comfort 2**

# RYHL (SPLASH POINT)

How To Get There

From Chester follow the old coast road A548 and as you come into Rhyl turn right at the second set of traffic lights onto the B5118. From here go straight down for ½ mile until the road turns left. This is Splash Point. Park your car here, but it is pay and display.

Grid Ref SJ 020823

How To Fish

From this venue it is possible to catch lots of Bass from 1-4lbs on ragworm and sandeel. Don't overcast for these as they are in the surf. Also in the summer you get Mackerel caught on feathers along with Doggies and Whiting. Also you will catch some good Plaice and Dabs to worm baits.

When the winter comes the Whiting get a lot bigger and when conditions are right you can catch some nice Codling to worm baits tipped with squid.

# RYHL (SPLASH POINT)

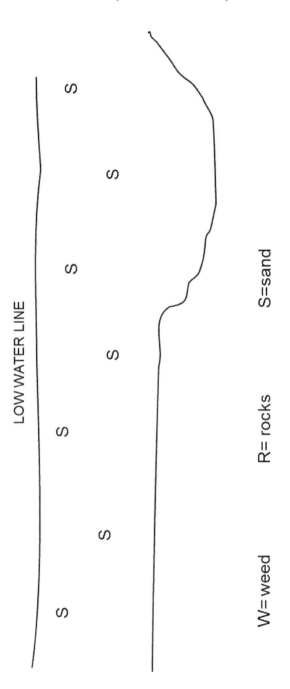

LOW WATER LINE

S  S  S  S  S  S  S

W= weed     R= rocks     S=sand

# RYHL (SPLASH POINT)

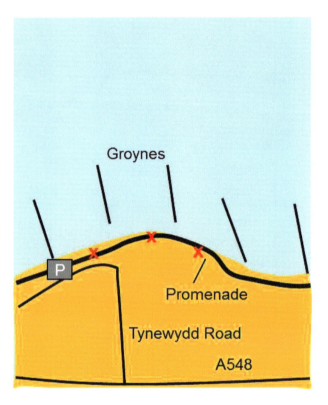

**Parking and Walking** …...Park on the road side (pay and display) and a 5 minute walk to the fishing.

**Summer Species** ………. Bass, Whiting, Plaice, Dabs, Mackerel, Doggies.

**Winter Species**……..….…..Codling, Whiting, Dabs, Flounder, Doggies.

**Best Months**……..……..…..June – Dec.

**Rigs** ………………..……..…. 2 and 3 hook Clip Down 1/0 with a rolling lead.

**Best Baits**……..…..............Lugworm, Ragworm, squid, mackerel, sandeel.

| Target the Bass here. |
| --- |

| Access 1    Comfort 1 |
| --- |

# KINMEL BAY

How To Get There

Follow the old coast road A548 from Rhyl for 2 ½ miles. Turn right at the traffic lights down Saint Asaph Avenue by Asda. Continue down this road to the car park at the end. From here the beach is just over the wall.

Grid Ref SH 987806

How To Fish

Here you have a sandy/pebble beach with not many snags. Bass are the main target but you need the textbook weather with a good surf and locate the Gullies to catch them. Using ragworm and sandeel you might be able to tempt specimens up to 6lbs. Also here you will catch Whiting and Doggies to fish baits and Flounder, Dabs and Plaice to worm baits. It is possible for some good Thornback Rays here on sandeel reaching up to 7lbs. In the winter you will get a run of codling up to 3-4lbs, and the usual larger Whiting and Doggies to fish baits.

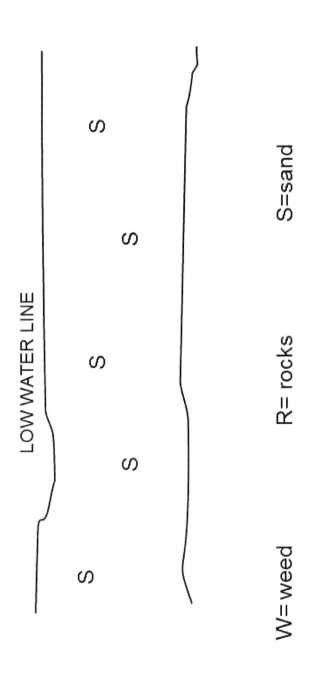

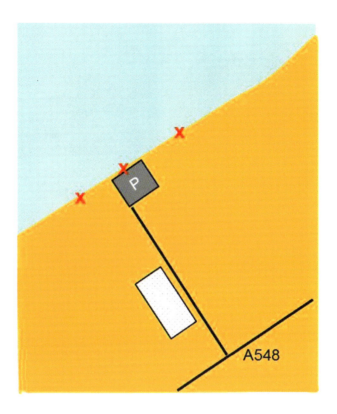

**Parking and Walking** …...Park in the car park and the fishing is a 2 minute walk.

**Summer Species** ………. Bass, Whiting, Plaice, Flounder, Dabs, Doggies, Thornback Rays.

**Winter Species**……..…….Codling, Whiting, Dabs, Flounder, Doggies.

**Best Months**……..……...Jul – Dec.

**Rigs** ……………..……..... 2 and 3 hook Clip Down 1/0 with a rolling lead, Pennel Pulley 2/0.

**Best Baits**……..…..........Lugworm, Ragworm, squid, mackerel, sandeel.

---

**Target the Bass here and look for the gullies.**

---

**Access 2    Comfort 2**

# PENSARN

How To Get There

Follow the old coast road A548 from Rhyl for 5 miles. When you get to the round about in Pensarn, take the 3$^{rd}$ turn off up Kingsway road and bear left. Go over the railway bridge and turn right. From here you have unlimited parking on the shingle beach. Fish from here.

Grid Ref SH 945787

How To Fish

A fantastic Bass Venue. This is a very steep shingle beach where only a short cast puts you in 30ft of water at high tide. Here you can catch lots of Bass to over 4lbs fishing the gullies in a good surf to lugworm, ragworm, sandeel and the odd one to spinners. If you wear chest waders and wade out you can reach another deep gully which holds decent size Bass. All this is great on light tackle. In the summer you can get Mackerel on feathers along with Whiting, Pollack and Doggies to fish baits. You will also get Dabs and Plaice to worm baits.

In the winter you get the run of Codling to 3lbs, the larger Whiting and still the odd Bass to worm and fish baits.

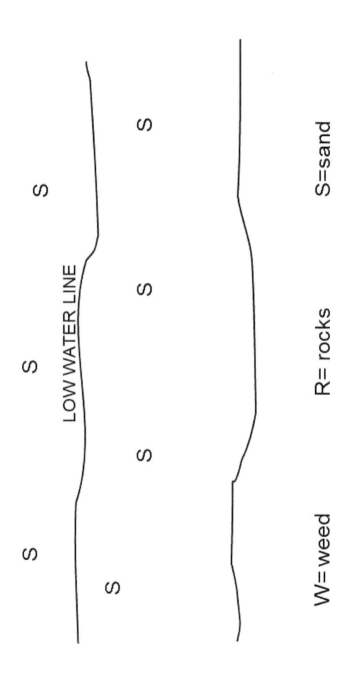

LOW WATER LINE

S

S

S

S

S

S

S=sand

R= rocks

W=weed

# PENSARN

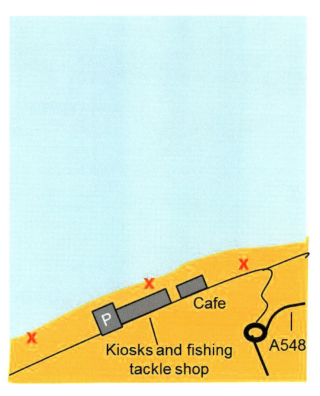

**Parking and Walking** …...Park on the shingle beach and fish anywhere from here.
**Summer Species** ………. Bass, Whiting, Pollack, Plaice, Dabs, Mackerel, Doggies.
**Winter Species**……...…….Codling, Whiting, Pollack, Dabs, Flounder, Doggies.
**Best Months**……..……...Jul – Feb.
**Rigs** ………….…….…...… 2 and 3 hook Clip Down 1/0  with a rolling lead, feathers, spinners.
**Best Baits**……..…..........Lugworm, Ragworm, squid, mackerel, sandeel.

Excellent venue for Bass, fishing the gullies with Lugworm.

**Access  2     Comfort  2**

# LLANDULLAS

How To Get There

Travel along the A55 and turn off at the Llandullas signpost. As you approach the roundabout, turn right down Wern Road. Follow this road for 100yds and turn left immediately after the caravan park. Go down this road, under the bridge to the car parks at the end. Fish anywhere from here but best by the river to the right.

Grid Ref SH 907786

How To Fish

Can fish well at low water but is best fished by the mouth of the river over high water with a good surf for the Bass, caught on lugworm, ragworm and sandeel with 6-7lbs possible. A lead lift is a must here over high tide due to the rock strewn beach close in. Also here you can catch some nice Conger to large fish baits and some good size Pollack.

In the winter you can expect some good Codling to 3lbs at night time caught on worm and squid cocktail. Conger Eel are often caught from here on a large fish bait. Also here you will catch Whiting, Doggies, Plaice, Dab and Flounder.

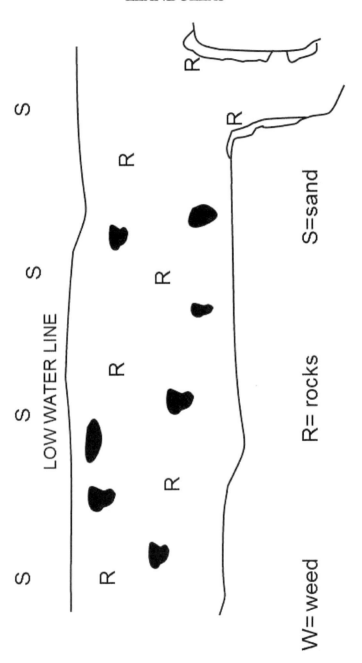

# LLANDULLAS

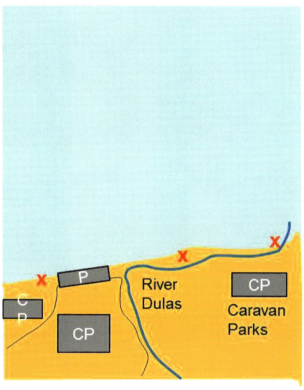

**Parking and Walking** …...From the car park follow the river to the second bridge and fish here. It is a ten minute walk.
**Summer Species** ……… Bass, Whiting, Plaice, Dabs, Mackerel, Doggies.
**Winter Species**……...……Codling, Whiting, Plaice, Dabs, Flounder, Doggies, Conger.
**Best Months**……..……...Sept - Feb.
**Rigs** ……………..…….....… 2 and 3 hook Clip Down 1/0, Conger Rig, Pulley Rig 5/0.
**Best Baits**………..….........Lugworm, Ragworm, squid, mackerel, sandeel.

---

Bass are the main target here.

---

**Access  2     Comfort  3**

# COLWYN BAY (THE ARCHES)

How To Get There

Travel along the A55 and turn off at the signpost for Old Colwyn. Go down the dip and turn right. At the T junction turn right again and follow this road all the way to the bottom where there is a small car park. At high tide you can fish from the car.

Grid Ref SH 9869787

How To Fish

In the summer you can get lots of Mackerel here at high tide on feathers. Great for the table or in the freezer for bait. This venue is good at both high and low tide with Mackerel to feathers, Whiting, Doggies to fish baits and Flatties to worm. Bass also put on a good show here and each year they used to have the Colwyn Bay Bass Festival.

In the winter the Whiting go very large at times and the Codling go to 3lbs to worm and squid cocktail. You can also catch Pollack, Rockling and large amounts of Dogfish caught on fish baits.

The Pier in Colwyn Bay has now closed and is not fishable but if you fish to the right of the Pier at low water with worm baits you can expect to catch plenty of School Bass. Also the new sea defence being erected in 2012 looks likely to be an outstanding fishing platform.

# COLWYN BAY (THE ARCHES)

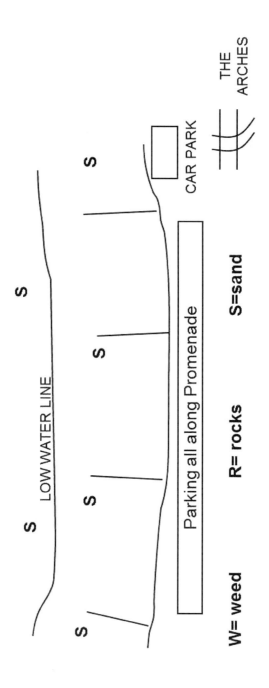

# COLWYN BAY (THE ARCHES)

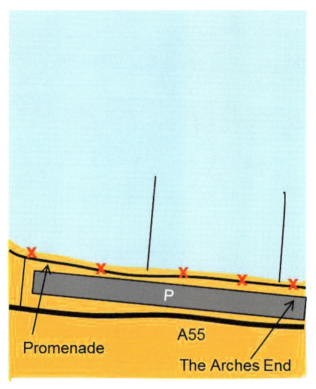

**Parking and Walking** …...park in the car park and fish from the promenade at high water.
**Summer Species** ………. Bass, Whiting, Plaice, Dabs, Mackerel, Doggies.
**Winter Species**……..…….Codling, Whiting, Dabs, Flounder, Doggies.
**Best Months**……..……...Jun – Feb.
**Rigs** ………….….……...… 2 and 3 hook Clip Down 1/0 with a rolling lead.
**Best Baits**…………........Lugworm, Ragworm, squid, mackerel, sandeel, crab.

---

**Excellent Whiting venue from October.**

---

**Access 1    Comfort 1**

# RHOS ON SEA

How To Get There

Travel along the A55 and turn off at the signpost For Old Colwyn. Go down the dip and turn right. At the T junction turn left and carry on for 1 ½ miles until you come into Rhos on Sea.

Grid Ref SH 842804

How To Fish

This is an excellent venue to fish when it is too rough at Colwyn Bay as it more sheltered. Here you get lots of Whiting and Dogfish to fish baits, Dabs and good sized Plaice to lug and ragworm. Bass can also be caught here using sandeel and ragworm.

When the winter arrives the Whiting get bigger and the Codling turn up reaching 4lbs, caught on worm and fish baits. The resident Doggies will eat anything you throw at them but best off using fish baits.

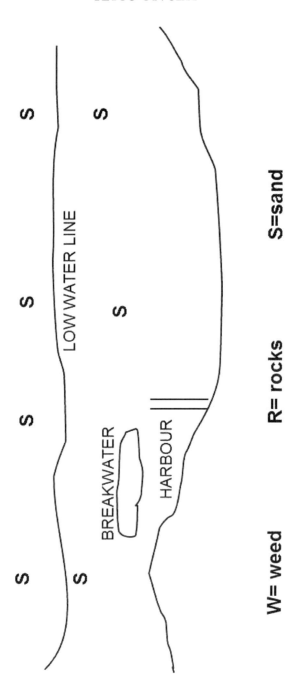

# RHOS ON SEA

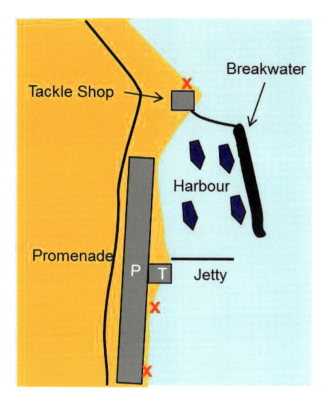

**Parking and Walking** …...Park on the roadside and fish next to your car.
**Summer Species** ………. Bass, Whiting, Plaice, Dabs, Mackerel, Doggies.
**Winter Species**……...…….Codling, Whiting, Dabs, Flounder, Doggies.
**Best Months**……...……..June – Dec.
**Rigs** ………………….…...… 2 and 3 hook Clip Down 1/0.
**Best Baits**………...…..........Lugworm, Ragworm, squid, mackerel, sandeel.

---

**A sheltered venue for winter Whiting.**

---

**Access 1    Comfort 1**

# PENRHYN BAY

How To Get There

Travel along the A55 and turn off at the signpost For Old Colwyn. Go down the dip and turn right. At the T junction turn left and carry on for 2 ½ miles. As you come in to Penrhyn you will see the bay on the right. Park here in the large lay bye.

Grid Ref SH 826816

How To Fish

One of my favourite places. Lovely views, great parking and fantastic fishing.

This venue can be fished at either low water or high. I personally prefer 2hrs before high to 2hrs after at night time. Bass are the main target here in the summer where they can reach 7-8lbs, caught in the right conditions on ragworm and sandeel baits. You can also catch Mackerel and Pollack on feathers or hokai lures, Whiting and Doggies on fish bait and Dabs to lugworm. Put a good cast out baited with sandeel or mackerel and you can expect some nice Thornback Rays.

In the winter you can get Codling in the 3-5lbs range, the bigger Whiting, the odd Bass and of course the ever present Dogfish.

# PENRHYN BAY

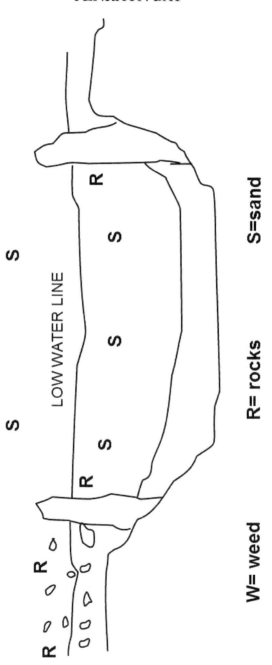

LOW WATER LINE

S=sand

R= rocks

W= weed

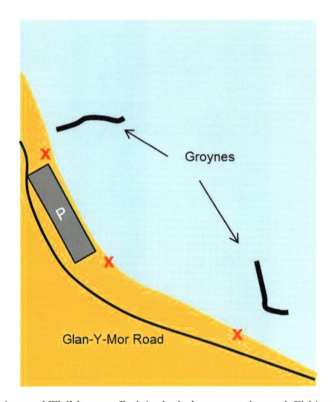

**Parking and Walking** …...Park in the layby next to the road. Fishing is a 2 minute walk.

**Summer Species** ………. Bass, Whiting, Plaice, Dabs, Pollack, Mackerel, Doggies, Gurnard, Thornback Rays.

**Winter Species**…….…..Codling, Whiting, Dabs, Flounder, Doggies, Bass, Gurnard, Rockling, Coalies.

**Best Months**……..……..Jul – Feb.

**Rigs** ………….…….....… 2 and 3 hook Clip Down 1/0, Pulley Rig 4/0, Conger rig.

**Best Baits**………..…..........Lugworm, Ragworm, squid, crab, mackerel, sandeel, feathers,          hokai lures.

> **Some very nice Bass can be caught from here.**

> **Access  2     Comfort 2**

46

# LLANDUDNO (ANGEL BAY)

How To Get There

Travel along the A55 and turn off at the signpost For Old Colwyn. Go down the dip and turn right. At the T junction turn left and carry on the B5115 for 3 miles. Take the last right before the roundabout down Shaftsbury Ave. When you get to the T junction turn left then immediate right down Penrhyn Beach. At the next junction turn left onto Penrhyn Beach West and follow this road all the way to the end. When you get there, park your car on the left . From here, go through the gate and bear right. Follow the footpath to the end and you have reached Angel Bay.

Grid Ref SH 818827

How To Fish

Angel Bay is treacherous when getting down in the wet. Be careful and don't fish this mark on your own.

Here the ground is quite rough, so expect to lose some tackle. Fishing the incoming tide with a good surf makes it ideal for some cracking Bass to sandeel and ragworm. Using a large fish bait you might be able to tempt one of the many Conger or Bullhuss that are caught here. Also you can expect to catch Whiting and Dogfish.

In the winter you get Codling to 4lbs on fish worm and squid baits, larger Whiting, Pollack and Coalies to fish baits. Also you will catch Doggies and Dabs.

# LLANDUDNO (ANGEL BAY)

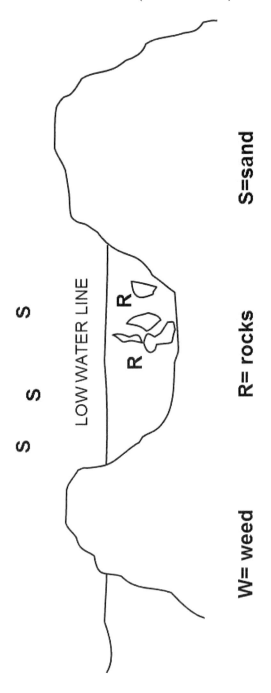

S=sand

R= rocks

W= weed

LOW WATER LINE

S    S

S    S

R    R

# LLANDUDNO (ANGEL BAY)

**Parking and Walking** …...Park by the gate and follow the footpath which is a ten minute walk.
**Summer Species** ………. Bass, Whiting, Bullhuss, Thornback Rays, Plaice, Dabs, Mackerel, Doggies.
**Winter Species**……...……Codling, Whiting, Dabs, Flounder, Doggies.
**Best Months**……..……..June – Dec.
**Rigs** ………….…….....… 2 and 3 hook Clip Down 1/0 with a rolling lead.
**Best Baits**………..….........Lugworm, Ragworm, squid, mackerel, sandeel.

Danger! A very steep climb down. Always fish with a partner.

Access 5    Comfort 5

# LLANDUDNO (NORTH SHORE)

How To Get There

Travel along the A55 and turn off at the signpost For Old Colwyn. Go down the dip and turn right. At the T junction turn left and carry on the B5115 for about 5 miles. As you enter Llandudno you can park your car on the roadside next to the beach. Park as close to the Little Orme as possible. It is better fishing here.

Grid Ref SH 804823

How To Fish

In the summer you will get plenty of Mackerel on feathers as they come in with the tide. Fishing the incoming tide will also produce some nice Bass to 5lbs, best caught on ragworm. Also here you will catch Plaice and Dabs to worm baits and Dogfish, Gurnard to fish baits. When the tide is in, be careful not to overcast and place your bait where the shingle meets the sand.

This place always fishes best in the winter with Whiting, Codling and Coalies being the main target caught on worm and fish baits. Flounder, Dabs and Dogfish are also on the menu along with the odd late Bass to ragworm and sandeel.

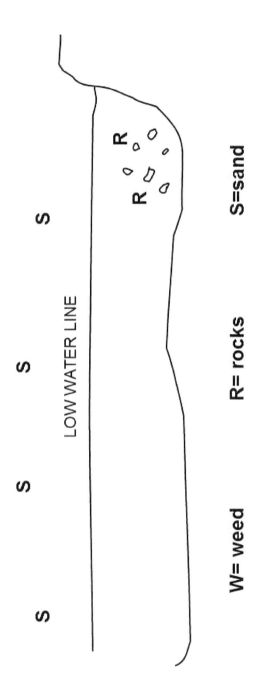

# LLANDUDNO (NORTH SHORE)

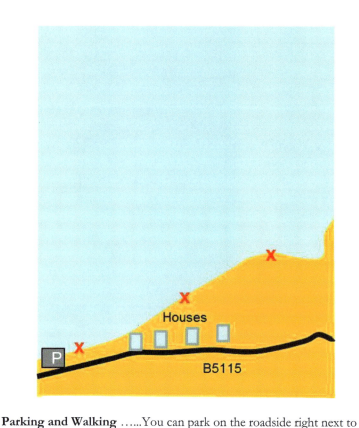

**Parking and Walking** …...You can park on the roadside right next to the beach.

**Summer Species** ………. Bass, Whiting, Plaice, Dabs, Mackerel, Doggies, Gurnard.

**Winter Species**…….…......Codling, Whiting, Dabs, Flounder, Doggies.

**Best Months**……..…….…..Jul – Feb.

**Rigs** …………….……....… 2  hook Clip Down 1/0.

**Best Baits**……….…............Lugworm, Ragworm, squid, mackerel, sandeel.

---

**Excellent venue for Mackerel in the summer.**

---

**Access  2     Comfort  2**

# LLANDUDNO (PIER)

How To Get There

Travel along the A55 and turn off at the signpost for Old Colwyn. Go down the dip and turn right. At the T junction turn left and carry on the B5115 for about 6 miles. When you get to the Pier, drive past and park to the left of Paddys tackle shop in the pay and display car park.

Grid Ref SH 783830

How To Fish

Fishing is now only allowed at the very end of the Pier and night time is best and always out fishes daytime.

This venue can produce very well all year round with Mackerel. Bass, Whiting, Dogfish, Pollack, Gurnard and Conger all being caught in the summer and a good run of Smoothhounds can be caught in the spring.

You can fish here with a variety of baits but don't forget to try the float with baited feathers and Hokai lures, these can sometimes work a treat.

In the winter you get Whiting, Coalies, Doggies, Conger and some good Codling up to 10lbs caught on lug and peeler crab. A drop net is required here with some big fish always being possible. A good cast of 100yds at 11:00 o'clock from the end puts you onto a nice sand bank where Plaice of 5lbs have been caught and also some good Thornback Rays to Sandeel.

# LLANDUDNO (PIER)

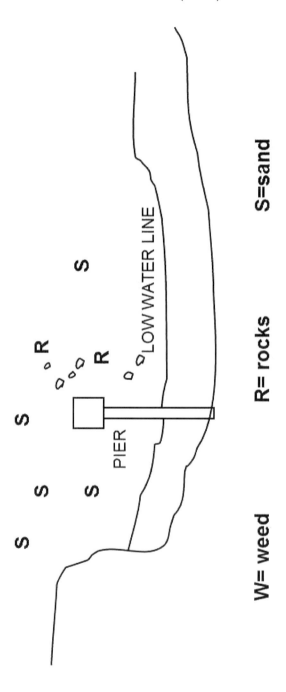

# LLANDUDNO (PIER)

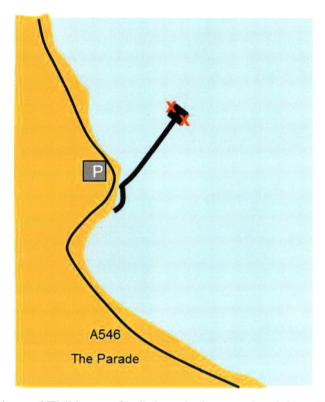

**Parking and Walking** …...Small charge in the car park and then a 10 minute walk to the end.

**Summer Species** ………. Bass, Whiting, Plaice, Dabs, Mackerel, Doggies, Pollack, Gurnard, Thornback Rays, Smoothhounds.

**Winter Species**……..……Codling, Whiting, Dabs, Flounder, Doggies, Conger, Plaice, Thornback Rays.

**Best Months**……..……..Sept – Feb.

**Rigs** ……………..……...… 2 and 3 hook Clip Down 1/0, Pulley Pennel 4/0, Conger Rig.

**Best Baits**……..…..........Lugworm, peeler crab, Ragworm, squid, mackerel, sandeel.

---

**Some nice size Conger Eels can be caught here.**

---

**Access  1    Comfort  1**

55

# LLANDUDNO (PIER) Rules

Llandudno sea fishing tackle and bait shop now known as PIER POINT tackle & bait Llandudno. The fishing rights are now owned and controlled by RHOS POINT sea fishing.

Times that the paid up member can fish the pier.
Fishing Platform Full Length of Pier
November / December / January / February / March 8 am till 2 am 6 pm till 2 am
May / June / July / August 8 am till 2 am 11.30 pm till 2 am
September 8 am till 2 am 10.30 pm till 2 am
October 8 am till 2 am 9 pm till 2 am

The membership price has now been **reduced** to £40.00 per year per person. **And the £15.00 joining fee has been removed/cancelled.**
2 x passport size photos required.
The night fishing sessions will be £25.00 for up to 12 anglers. 6pm till 2am but negotiations are on going to up this to all night sessions
Day ticket fishing is now £4.00 per rod with a limited amount of rods allowed this is to allow for season ticket membership holders who will have priority.
For further information please contact Rhos Point Sea Fishing shop at Rhos point Colwyn bay
email; contacts@rhospointpathfinder.com                     or call 07719 556 092.

# LLANDUDNO (PIER) Rules

1. These rules must be taken into account when applying for season ticket/membership.
2. No petrol/ paraffin lamps / cookers permitted on the pier at any time.
3. No damaging of the pier or property of the pier including woodwork/paint work etc and barbecues.
4. No alcohol to be consumed on the pier except any that has been purchased from the pier bar.
5. All litter must be put in the bins provided or taken home with you.
6. No fishing behind the kiosks up and down the pier.
7. No fishing on the narrow section of the pier (from the tackle shop down to the main pier entrance.)
8. If you misbehave or break these rules you run the real risk of being evicted from the pier and your membership being cancelled without any refund.
9. Rhos point/pier point and the pier owners reserve the right to change any of these rules without negotiation.
10. Children under the age of 16 must be accompanied by an adult.
11. There will be competition from time to time on the pier so your patience would be appreciated.
12. There will be a charge for gate keys ( at cost ) Lost replacement keys charged for at cost. If membership is not renewed key must be retuned and a refund will be given.
13. Night fishing could include 2 parties of up to 12 anglers (pre booked)

# LLANDUDNO (PIGEON HOLES)

How To Get There

Travel along the A55 and turn off at the signpost for Old Colwyn. Go
down the dip and turn right. At the T junction turn left and carry on the
B5115 for about 6 miles. When get into Llandudno drive past the Pier
and up the hill. Go through the gate house (£2.50 in season) and up on
the Orme. Follow this road and pull in at the layby by the 2nd seating
bench on the right. Walk through the gap in the wall and down the rocky
slope to the rock platforms at the bottom. Be careful down this slope, it
is very slippery in the wet.

Grid Ref SH 779838

How To Fish

Fishing can be superb here. You have got excellent rock platforms with
good footing and deep water very close in. With this in mind, a long cast
is not necessary. You can reap this venue in the summer by float fishing
for Wrasse and Pollack or spinning for the Bass. Peeler crab reigns
supreme here with Bullhuss being a good target, my personal best being
12 1/2lbs. Mackerel are also caught here by the bucket load, fantastic on
light tackle fishing with feathers.

In winter the Codling to 10lbs arrive with the Coalies caught on fish and
worm baits. Conger Eels always put in a show up to 20lbs in weight, best
caught on a mackerel flapper. Also here the Doggies are in abundance
along with good size Whiting caught on fish baits.

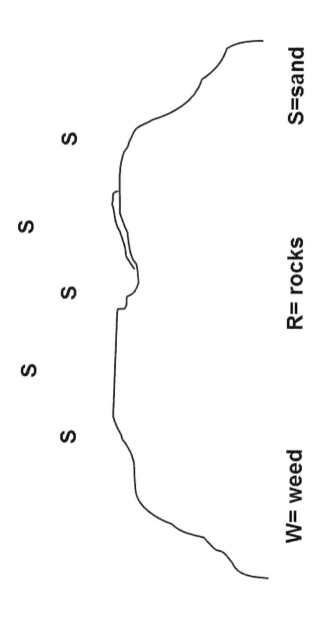

S=sand

R= rocks

W= weed

S S S S S

# LLANDUDNO (PIGEON HOLES)

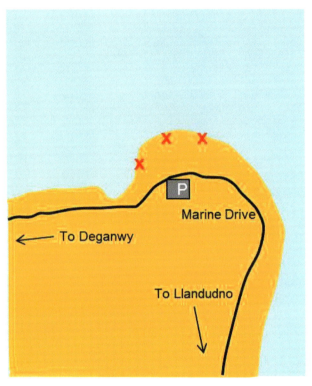

**Parking and Walking** …...Park in the layby by the second seat. Walk through the gap in the wall and down the slope to the rock platforms.
**Summer Species** ………. Bass, Whiting, Plaice, Dabs, Mackerel, Doggies.
**Winter Species**……...……..Codling, Whiting, Dabs, Flounder, Doggies.
**Best Months**……...………..June – Feb.
**Rigs** ………………..……...… 2 Clip Down 1/0
**Best Baits**………...…...........Lugworm, Ragworm, squid, mackerel, sandeel.

---

Danger! A steep climb down and very slippery in the wet.

---

Access  4    Comfort  4

# DEGANWY

How To Get There

Come off the A55 at the Deganwy sign post on to the A546 Glan Y Mor Road. Follow this road and as you enter Deganwy, turn left in to Marine Crescent. Drive down this road to the end and park your car. Fish where the river starts to open wider or a little further to the mouth of the Conwy Estuary.

Grid Ref SH 775792

How To Fish

The best mark here would have to be fishing over the mussel beds which are just inside the mouth of the Conwy estuary. Bass are the target with peeler crab and lugworm being the best baits.

Fished 2hrs either side of low water on the big spring tides produces the best results. Also caught here in the summer are Codling, Thornback Rays and the ever present Flatties which are caught throughout the tide using worm and fish as bait.

In the Winter the Codling get bigger with the occasional double figure fish showing up. The hoards of Whiting and Doggies will eat just about everything and should keep you busy.

A long cast is not necessary here and 15 – 30 yards will put you amongst the fish. The Flounder can be right in at the sides .

You will also need 5oz and 6oz to combat the strong tidal flow and big clumps of weed after a strong blow.

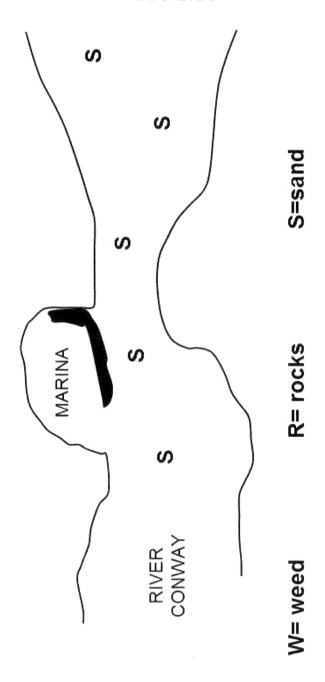

S=sand

R= rocks

W= weed

MARINA

RIVER CONWAY

# DEGANWY

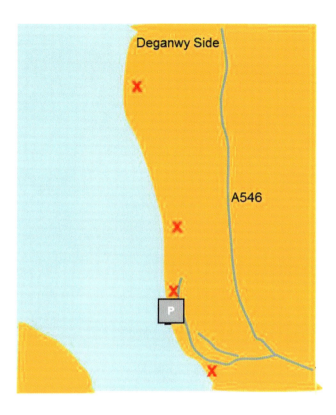

**Parking and Walking** …...Park at the bottom of Marina Crescent and fish from here.

**Summer Species** ………. Bass, Plaice, Dabs, Flounder, Silver Eels.

**Winter Species**……...…….Codling, Whiting, Dabs, Flounder, Doggies, Sea Trout.

**Best Months**……..……..Sept – Dec.

   **Rigs** …………..……...…. 2 and 3 hook Flapper 1/0 with a rolling lead.

**Best Baits**……..……..........Crab, Lugworm, Ragworm, Sandeel, Fish Baits.

---

Good venue for Bass and Flatties.

---

**Access 2    Comfort 2**

# CONWAY MARINA

How To Get There

Drive down the A55 and turn off at the Conway Marina sign post. Follow this road until you get to the T junction and turn right on to Ellis Road. Carry on to the end where you can park our car and fish from here.

Grid Ref SH 777786

How To Fish

This venue is fishing the River Conway. Although this venue blows hot and cold it is well worth a mention when the weather is too rough for the beaches as this is nice and sheltered. Crab baits reign supreme over all other baits here with ragworm coming second. In the summer you can catch Bass to 4lbs on crab and rag, and Plaice, Dabs, and Flounder to worm. Sometimes Silver Eels can become a pest.

In the winter you still get the odd Bass but Codling are the most sort after. Also here you will get plenty of Whiting and Dogfish to fish baits and also the occasional Sea Trout.

# CONWAY MARINA

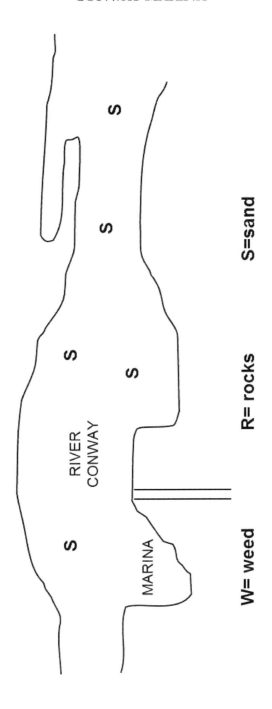

# CONWAY MARINA

**Parking and Walking** …....Park at the end of Ellis Road and fish from here.

**Summer Species** ………. Bass, Plaice, Dabs, Flounder, Silver Eels.

**Winter Species**……...…....Codling, Whiting, Dabs, Flounder, Doggies, Sea Trout.

**Best Months**……..……...Sept – Dec.

**Rigs** …………….……...… 2 and 3 hook Flapper 1/0 with a rolling lead.

**Best Baits**…………..…..........Crab, Ragworm, Fish Baits.

---

**Very sheltered venue when it's too rough elsewhere.**

---

**Access 2    Comfort 2**

# PENMAENMAWR

How To Get There

Turn left off the A55 as you come towards Penmaenmawr onto Ffordd Conwy Road. Continue to drive on until you come to a T junction. Turn right here onto Pant-Yr-Afon, leading onto Ffordd Bangor Road. You will have to follow this road until you come to the flyover where you turn right. Go over the flyover and park by the beach.

Grid Ref SH 710762

How To Fish

A nice shallow sloping sand and shingle beach best fished on an incoming tide with a good surf. In the summer you can concentrate on the Bass fishing here and over the years you will see some good results. Caught mainly on ragworm and sandeel to around 4lbs. Thornback Rays can be caught at distance here on mackerel and sandeel baits along with plenty of Doggies and Whiting.

In the winter fish when it's rough and you can expect some Codling to 3lbs best caught on crab and lugworm. Also here you will catch the larger Whiting and Coalies to fish baits.

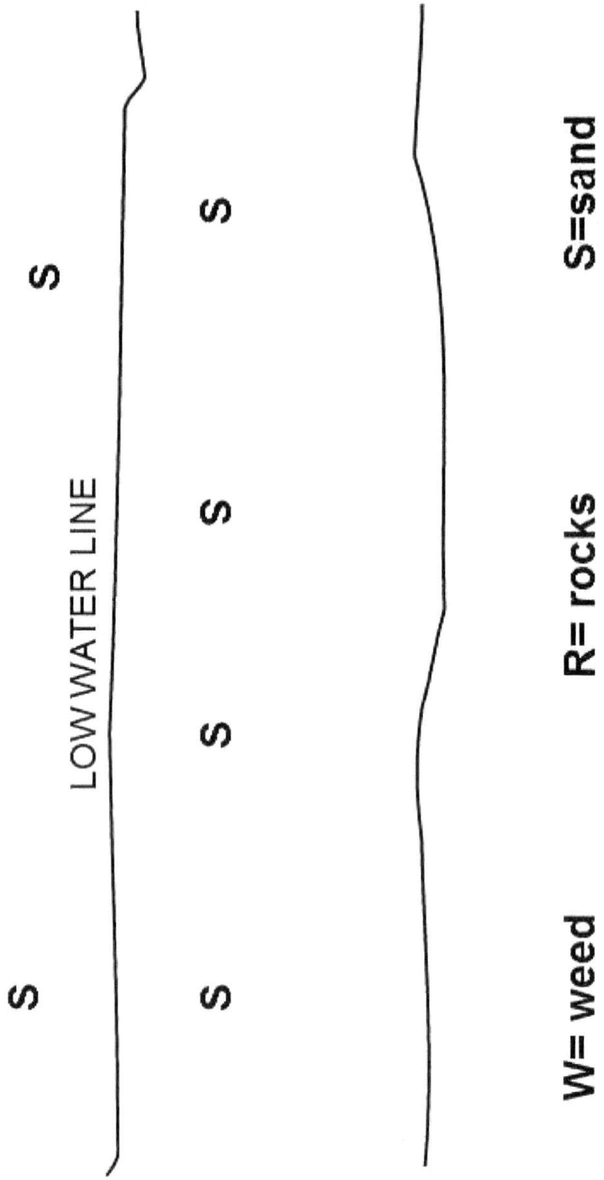
S
S
S
S
S
S
LOW WATER LINE
S=sand
R= rocks
W= weed

# PENMAENMAWR

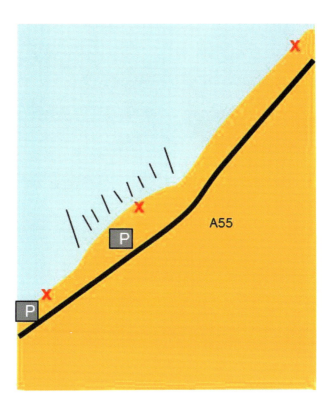

**Parking and Walking** …...Park on the promenade right next to the beach.

**Summer Species** ………. Bass, Whiting, Plaice, Dabs, Mackerel, Doggies.

**Winter Species**…….....…….Codling, Whiting, Dabs, Flounder, Doggies.

**Best Months**……..………..June – Dec.

**Rigs** ……………..……...… 2 and 3 hook Clip Down 1/0 with a rolling lead.

**Best Baits**…………...........Lugworm, Ragworm, squid, mackerel, sandeel.

---

### Look for the gullies to find the Bass.

---

### Access 2    Comfort 2

# LLANFAIRFECHAN

How To Get There

Come off the A55 at the Llanfairfechan round about. Turn right down Penmaenmawr Road and follow this until you come to the crossroads. Turn right here down Station Road and carry on until you reach the promenade. You can park your car and fish from here.

Grid Ref SH 681751

How To Fish

Another shallow sloping sand and shingle beach, very similar to Penmaenmawr.  Bass again are the main target in the summer. Try not to over cast as these are in the surf and patrolling the gullies. Use sandeel, lugworm and crab for these. Dabs and Flounder are always caught here using worms as bait. Another good bait here are razor fish as these are abundant to the area.

In the winter the Codling arrive, coming in at about 4lbs, caught on lug and squid cocktails. Whiting and Dogfish are in abundance along with a good run of Coalies in February

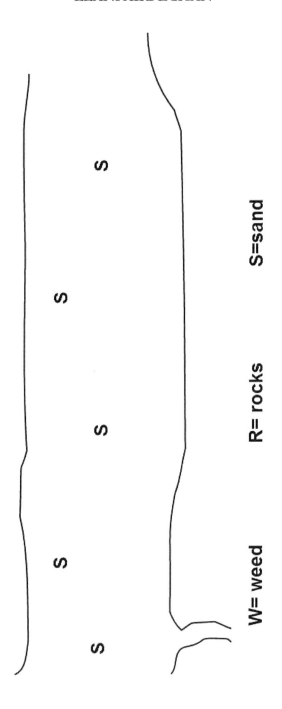

# LLANFAIRFECHAN

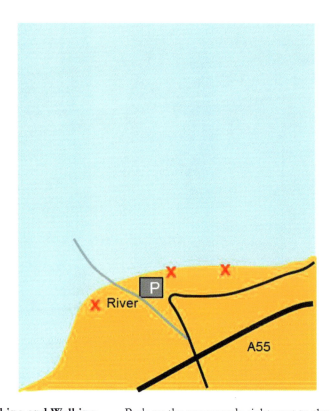

**Parking and Walking** …... Park on the promenade right next to the beach.

**Summer Species** ………. Bass, Whiting, Plaice, Dabs, Mackerel, Doggies.

**Winter Species**……..…..….Codling, Whiting, Dabs, Flounder, Doggies.

**Best Months**……..……….June – Dec.

**Rigs** ………………..…..… 2 and 3 hook Clip Down 1/0 with a rolling lead.

**Best Baits**………..…..........Lugworm, Ragworm, Razorfish, Squid, Mackerel, Sandeel.

---

Excellent venue for Bass, fishing the gullies with Lugworm.

---

Access 2    Comfort 2

# PORT PENRHYN DOCK

How To Get There

Turn right off the A55 onto the A5 at the Snowdon and Menai Strait roundabout. Follow the A5 for about 2 miles and turn right at the Porth Penrhyn sign post. Follow this road over the river and towards the scrap yard ahead. Turn left just before the scrap yard and travel for 100yds where you can park your car and fish.

Grid Ref SH 592728

How To Fish

This is an excellent venue, but there is a very fast tidal run here which at times can make fishing difficult with the amount of weed that it brings along. Bass are again the main target here with these silver bars best being caught on crab, sandeel or razorfish. There are lots of weaver fish caught here so be careful what you grab hold of. Also here you will catch Whiting, Doggies and Codling.

When winter comes you can expect plenty of Codling to 6lbs on lugworm and squid cocktail and a good run of Coalies from November onwards. You will also get the Whiting and Doggies to fish baits and Flounder and Plaice to worm baits.

# PORT PENRHYN DOCK

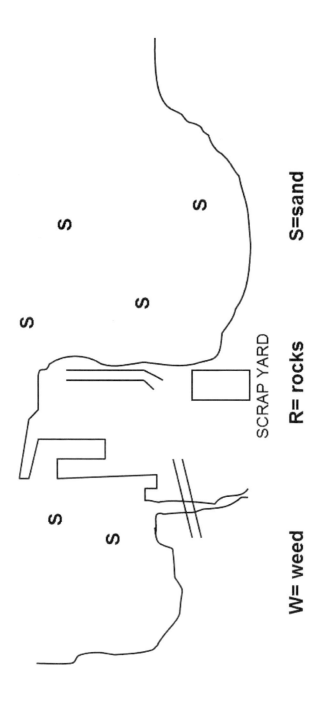

# PORT PENRHYN DOCK

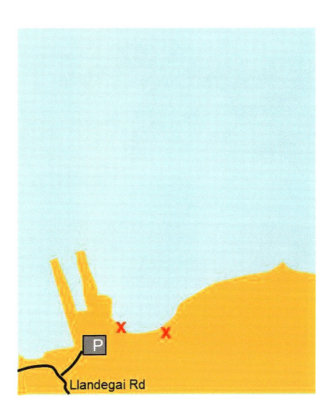

**Parking and Walking** …...Turn left before the scrap yard. Park your car and fish from here.

**Summer Species** ………. Bass, Codling, Whiting, Plaice, Dabs, Doggies.

**Winter Species**……...…….Codling, Whiting, Dabs, Flounder, Doggies.

**Best Months**……..……...May - Feb.

**Rigs** …………..………...… 2 and 3 hook Flapper 1/0 with a rolling lead.

**Best Baits**…………...........Lugworm, Ragworm, razorfish, squid, mackerel, sandeel.

---

**Bass are the main target here.**

---

**Access 2    Comfort 2**

# BANGOR PIER

How To Get There

Turn right off the A55 onto the A5 at the Snowdon and Menai Strait roundabout. Follow the A5 for about 3 miles and turn right just after Dickies Boats down Snowdon and Menai Strait Road. This road leads to the car park in front of the Pier.

Grid Ref SH 584729

How To Fish

A very comfortable place to fish with plenty of cover if the weather is bad. Fishing at night time costs £12 for a group and you get the tickets from the Pier house by the entrance.

There is plenty of room at the end of the pier for plenty of anglers .
A very good venue with lots of different varieties of fish to be caught. In the summer you will be able to catch Bass, Codling, Pollack, Gurnard, Dabs, Flounder and Doggies, all to worm and fish baits.

In the winter the Codling get bigger running up to 10lbs best caught on crab and lugworm tipped with squid. Also you get a good run of Coalies to about 3lbs on fish baits along with the ever present Dogfish. All in all, this is a cracking venue best fished at night time in the winter.

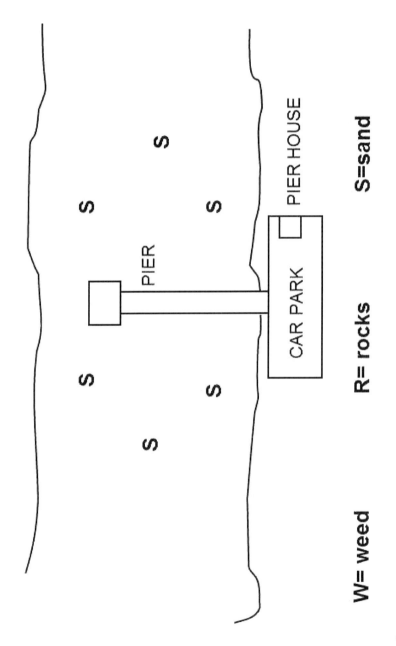

# BANGOR PIER

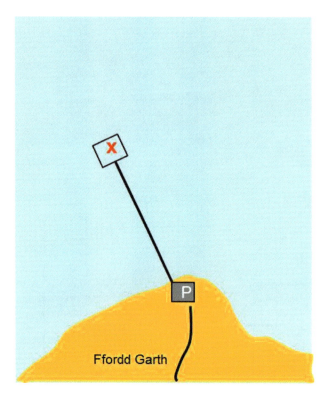

**Parking and Walking** …...Use the car park in front of the Pier at £1 cost. 10 minute walk to the end of the Pier.

**Summer Species** ………. Bass, Whiting, Plaice, Dabs, Mackerel, Doggies.

**Winter Species**……..…….Codling, Whiting, Dabs, Flounder, Doggies.

**Best Months**……..……..May – Feb.

**Rigs** …………….…….....… 2 and 3 hook Clip Down 1/0, Pennel Pulley 4/0.

**Best Baits**……..…..............Lugworm, Ragworm, Razorfish, Squid, Mackerel, Sandeel.

---

**Excellent venue for winter Cod.**

---

**Access 1    Comfort 1**

MUSCLE

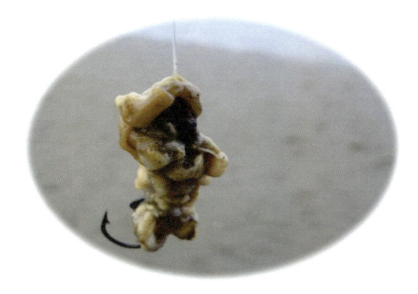

BASS

OCTOPUS

POLLACK

# BULLHUSS

# DOGFISH

# HORSE MACKEREL

# POUTING

# WHITING

# SILVER EEL

# CODLING

# ROCKLING

MACKEREL

BLACK BREAM

# CORKWING WRASSE

# DAB

Bait

**Mackerel** (Scomber scombrus) - This is probably the most important bait that you will ever use. It is an extremely oily fish and gives off a very strong scent in the water that attracts virtually every species of fish from both boat and shore.

It can be cut into strips for catching the smaller fish such as Whiting and Pollack, or can be used as a larger bait on a Pennel Rig for the winter Codling and Coalies. It can also be used as a Flapper on a 9/0 hook with a strong trace for Conger and Tope.

# Bait

**Ragworm**  (Hediste diversicolor) - In general there are two types of Ragworm used for sea fishing of which King Rag, is the largest.

The Ragworm you buy from the tackle shops is smaller and very often of the farmed variety which is an excellent bait for Cod, Wrasse and Bass.

Beware of the pincers on the larger worms as they can give you quite a nip.

Bait

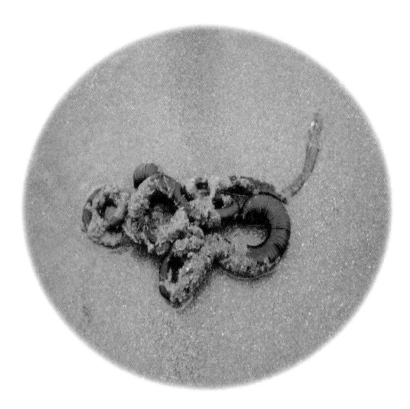

**Black Lugworm** (Arenicola defodiens) – These worms live right on the low water line and are best dug for on a large spring tide. Nowadays people more often than not use a bait pump instead of a spade for digging these out of the sand. Although still back aching, a pump is a lot easier than a spade.

Known as an exceptional bait for most species including Cod, where you would tip them off with squid or mackerel.

**Blow Lugworm** (Arenicola defodiens) **-** These are found in large numbers on the beach where you see a Cast with a Blow Hole next to it. You will have to be careful if using a Bait Pump as these live in a curved hole as opposed to the black Lugworm which live in a straight hole. With this being the case they are often dug for with a spade.

Again these are in general a great bait for most species, in some cases being tipped off with Squid or Mackerel.

**<u>Peeler Crab</u>** (Carcinus maenas) **-** These get their name from the fact that they molt and shed their skin at many stages throughout their life.

This bait reigns supreme and out fishes all other baits at certain times of the year. Peeler Crab gives off a very strong scent in the water  and is extremely effective when fishing for Cod, Bass, and Rays. It is also a great bait when fished under a float amongst the rocks and the weeds for large Wrasse.

**Squid** (Loligo Japonica) **-** Bought as Calamari from the supermarkets. This bait is great when used whole for Cod and Bass and is very effective when used in strips for tipping off worm baits. With this being a very tough bait it can be cast very long distances without being held on with bait elastic.

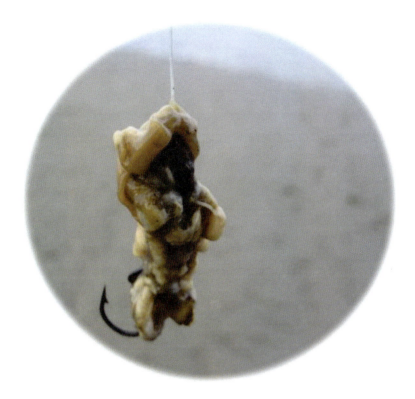

### Common Mussel

They are typically found in the intertidal zone either in crevices or on exposed rocks. They are commonly found in groups, known as mussel beds, and are capable of withstanding strong waves by means of their byssus thread attachments. A very under used but excellent bait, especially for Flatfish.

**Razor Fish**  (Ensis siliqua) – To collect Razor Fish you will have to prepare a heavily saturated solution of salt water. Half fill boiling water into a bottle with a squirty type lid and keep adding salt until no more will dissolve.

Find a sandy beach and look for dimples with a keyhole shape in the sand. From here you squirt the salty solution down the hole and this will cause the Razor Fish to lift from the hole. Alternatively you can tip a good quantity of cooking salt direct over the hole.

At this point gently but firmly take hold of the shell and gently pull from the sand. You can now put the Razor fish into a bucket of sea water which will keep fresh for a few days.

Because this is a soft bait you will have to use bait elastic to keep it on the hook when casting.

In my opinion, this is a very under used bait but is excellent for Cod, Bass, Flounder, Whiting and Dogfish.

# INDEX

| | |
|---|---|
| 36 | LLANDULLAS |
| 37 | LLANDULLAS |
| 38 | COLWYN BAY (THE ARCHES) |
| 39 | COLWYN BAY (THE ARCHES) |
| 40 | COLWYN BAY (THE ARCHES) |
| 41 | RHOS ON SEA |
| 42 | RHOS ON SEA |
| 43 | RHOS ON SEA |
| 44 | PENRHYN BAY |
| 45 | PENRHYN BAY |
| 46 | PENRHYN BAY |
| 47 | LLANDUDNO (ANGEL BAY) |
| 48 | LLANDUDNO (ANGEL BAY) |
| 49 | LLANDUDNO (ANGEL BAY) |
| 50 | LLANDUDNO (NORTH SHORE) |
| 51 | LLANDUDNO (NORTH SHORE) |
| 52 | LLANDUDNO (NORTH SHORE) |
| 53 | LLANDUDNO PIER |
| 54 | LLANDUDNO PIER |
| 55 | LLANDUDNO PIER |
| 56 | LLANDUDNO PIER RULES |
| 57 | LLANDUDNO PIER RULES |
| 58 | LLANDUDNO (PIGEON HOLES) |
| 59 | LLANDUDNO (PIGEON HOLES) |
| 60 | LLANDUDNO (PIGEON HOLES) |
| 61 | DEGANWY |
| 62 | DEGANWY |
| 63 | DEGANWY |
| 64 | CONWAY MARINA |
| 65 | CONWAY MARINA |
| 66 | CONWAY MARINA |
| 67 | PENMAENMAWR |
| 68 | PENMAENMAWR |
| 69 | PENMAENMAWR |
| 70 | LLANFAIRFECHAN |

# R.N.L.I

**Rhyl** was named the busiest lifeboat station in Wales for 2008 for the 5th year running with volunteer crews launching 79 times and rescuing 69 people.

Every year there are a few people (some anglers) who get washed of the rocks by rogue waves and swept out to sea. Many do not come back alive.

Some people are unaware of the dangers and the phenomenal power the sea has. When you go out fishing be prepared with the correct clothing and travel with someone who knows the area.

Please remember - when you put your life in danger, the lifeboat crews put their life on the line to save yours. These chaps are volunteers !!

**Please support the R.N.L.I. - they support you !**

## www.seafishingvenues.net
# The Home to Sea Fishing in Wales